INTRODUCTION

Can we all agree that the COVID pandemic opened doors we didn't know were there??!! Like starting passive income, working from home, side hustles, and so much more! This new age of technology has presented us with so many new ways to earn money and grow wealth with or WITHOUT a 9-5 rat race. The gig economy and side hustle culture has truly changed our access to and the way we make money.

There may come a time where we may need extra funds to make ends meet or save for a large purchase. That used to mean getting a a second job, working overtime, selling your possessions, what ever you had to do to get some extra income.

Today, if you need extra money, you can get a side hustle, and your side hustle options are literally limitless. And guess what? Car sharing with Turo is one of the awesome side hustles that can potentially become a 6-figure passive income business.

TABLE OF CONTENTS

01 **WHAT IS PEER TO PEER SHARING?**

02 **KNOW YOUR MARKET**

03 **HOW TO CHOOSE A VEHICLE**

04 **LIST YOUR VEHICLE ON TURO**

05 **TURO HOST PROTECTION PLAN OPTIONS**

06 **GETTING YOUR CAR ON THE ROAD**

07 **RETURNING THE VEHICLE**

08 **CAR SHARING BUSINESS EXPENSE**

09 **TURO MUST HAVES**

10 **PROMOTING YOUR BUSINESS OFF THE TURO APP**

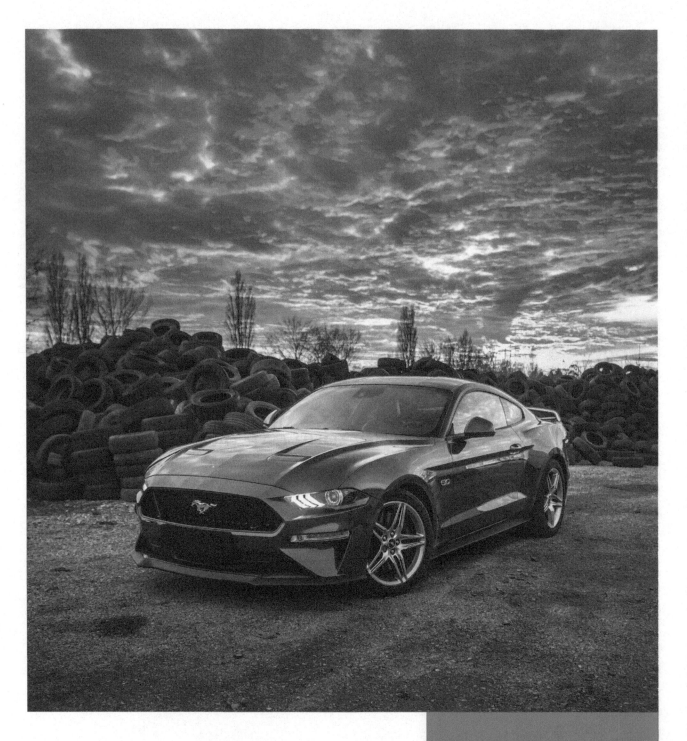

CHAPTER 1

WHAT IS
Peer To Peer
Car Sharing?

So, what is peer to peer car sharing? If you don't know what this is, let me explain.

Car sharing allows you to rent out your personal car to others while making money in return.

Are you familiar with traditional rental car companies like Hertz, Avis, or Enterprise? Peer-to-peer car sharing is a business model along these same lines. The only difference is you rent out your personal vehicle (or a fleet of vehicles) on an app like Turo.

This is an alternative to a traditional rental car company and gives customers other options outside of the more traditional avenues like Avis, Enterprise, or even Hertz.

Renting out your own vehicle is not the only option to getting started in this business, here are some other ways to start your business.

1 Owner

This is the most common and basic way to get started with peer-to-peer car sharing. The owner of the vehicle allows others to rent for short and long-term rentals.

2 Joint Venture

A joint venture is an agreement by two or more people or companies to accomplish a specific business goal together leveraging the other's cash or credit.

If you intend to own the vehicle jointly, you'll need a written agreement outlining the details and both names on the car's title.

3 Third Party

This type of business is a little different, you'd be responsible for marketing and managing the day-to-day operations of the owner's vehicles. In other words, the vehicles do not belong to you, you are simply managing the day-to-day operations for the business.

4 Co-Sharing

Lastly, co-sharing. Co-sharing consists of renting another person's existing car that is being underutilized and renting it out for a higher price. You would then give the owner a percentage or cut of the profits.

KNOW
Your Market

CHAPTER 2

Who Is Your Target Customer?

Before you purchase a car, you should understand who your target customer is going to be. This is because your target customer will greatly dictate what type of car you should get and what type of car does well on the Turo marketplace in your area.

Who Is Your Target Customer?

Here are a couple of questions you'll want to ask yourself:

1. Who is going to be renting your car?
2. Who do you want to rent your car?

Some examples would be:
- If your target is families on vacation who want to rent your car on a holiday, maybe a large SUV could be a good choice.
- If your target is people traveling to your city for work-related reasons, a more economical car like a 4-door sedan would be appropriate.
- If your target audience is renting your car to take to the beach for a nice day of fishing you would probably want a 4-wheel drive truck, SUV, or crossover.

Knowing your market and what your customers need will help you choose what type of car will do well in your area and what cars people will rent.

The point isn't just to list a car on Turo. You want people to rent your car, and that will never happen if your car is impractical for your area or city.

HOW TO
Choose a Vehicle

CHAPTER 3

Once you know what type of car you should get, you'll need to find a car to buy. I'll try to discuss everything you need to know about buying a car for Turo in this next section.

NEW OR USED?

New Or Used?

The **BIG** question is whether to buy new or used. I'm always asked what my opinion is. I will always recommend you do what works best for you and your market, but in this ebook, I will discuss what makes sense to me and my perspective. Of course, I'll provide statistics as well.

When it comes to buying a car for Turo, regardless of what "type" of car you buy, it's important to not buy a **new** car to list on Turo. The overall reason is simple: the depreciation will kill you and your business.... well that's my personal opinion.

When you buy a car for Turo, it is very important to buy a car at the lowest possible point in the depreciation curve.

New Or Used?

This is a standard depreciation curve for a vehicle (or course, there are exceptions to this rule):

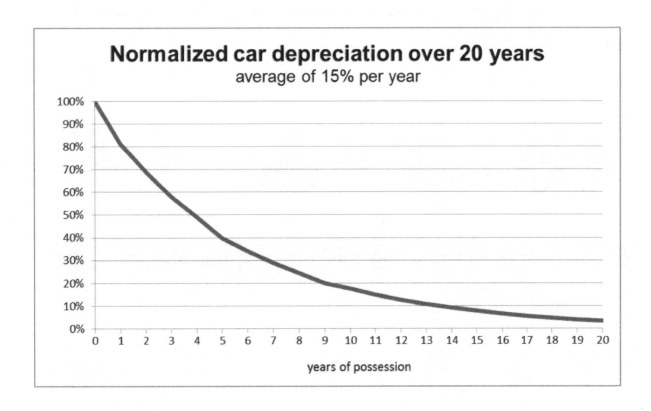

A car takes the biggest hit to its value in the first year of ownership, we are talking close to 20%. That means when you buy a new car, the second you drive it off the dealer's lot, that car will be worth 20% LESS than what you paid for it (not including the interest you'll be paying if financed with an interest rate).

New Or Used?

We need an exit strategy and that begins with making sure we don't lose when we need to sell. We want our cars to be worth MORE than what we pay for them. So, how do you do that? Well, I'll explain.

You want to make sure that the price you get for the car and your earnings from the car exceed the price you paid and any maintenance expenses. That's how you make money renting the car and then selling the car!

New Or Used?

So, how do we achieve this?

If you look at the curve, you'll see that after around the 7th year, the depreciation starts to slow down. Once we hit the depreciation bottom, the year-by-year depreciation has drastically declined.

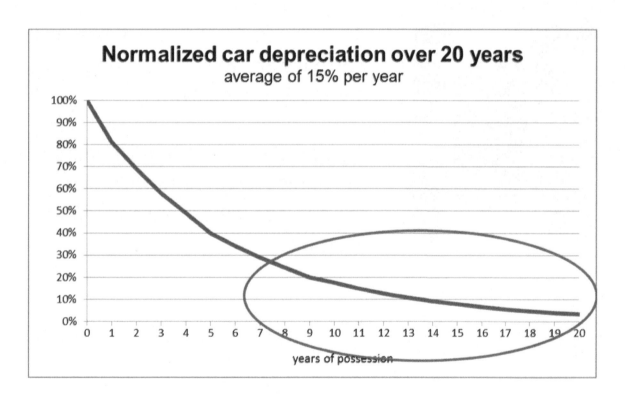

Normalized car depreciation over 20 years
average of 15% per year

QUICK TIPS

The first 5 years of a car's life are where it loses the majority of its value. After it has hit the depreciating bottom, the car retains its value much better. When your car exceeds the mileage or age requirement or if maintenance costs become too much, you will want to sell the car.

The Search Begins!

Now that we have depreciation down, where do we look for the car?

You'll want to check out websites like Facebook Marketplace, Craigslist, Offerup, local dealerships, Carvana, vroom, etc. I normally like to search listings that are made by the owner.

A good rule of thumb for finding the depreciation bottom is seeing the average lowest price you find for the car.

The Search Begins!

- You may see an older Honda vehicle listed for $10,000.
- You may see a lot of these Hondas listed for $10,000.
- Some are in better condition than others, some are maybe a year or two older, and some may have higher mileage, but it seems like regardless of the condition, the lowest you can find this car priced at is around $10,000.

This is a good indicator that the depreciation bottom for this car is $10,000, and if you can buy this car at this price, you are getting a pretty good deal.

The Search Begins!

In addition to buying cars at their depreciation bottom, it is also important to buy cars that are below the market value. Market value is the price of a car on average in any given market.

Just because a car has reached its depreciation bottom does not mean you're going to be getting a good deal on the car. That's where market value comes into play.

To determine the market value, you can use resources like Kelley Blue Book or even simply do your own market research. To do market research, all you have to do is go online to various websites and look up the specific type of car you are looking for.

The Search Begins!

Here Are Some Questions You Should Ask Yourself:

- What's the advertised price?

- Is this above or below the average price for this model and year?

- What would be considered a good deal?

Before you go to buy your car, you should know how much the average price for that car in your market is, you should know how much you expect to pay for the car, and you should know what fair market value is.

To get the best deal, you'll want to try to pay below the market value. That is setting yourself up to lose money later on down the road.

Inspect It First!

Finally! You found the car you want to purchase. Now it's time to check the car in person.

Here are some things you'll want to do prior to purchasing the car:

1 **Run The CarFax**
This is EXTREMELY IMPORTANT. Running the CarFax will allow you to see the maintenance the car has had and any or all accident history of the vehicle. You will learn how many miles the car should have (there have been times where the mileage indicated on the dashboard is much lower than it should be). It will also tell you how many owners the car has had and the status of the title. These are all critical things to know before buying a vehicle and running the CarFax is a necessary step of the buying process. In order to run the CarFax, all you need to do is ask the seller for the VIN or vehicle identification number and then go to CarFax.com and buy the report. The cost is relatively low, but it is a worthwhile investment for your Turo side hustle.

Inspect It First!

You've run the CarFax! Now it's time to meet the seller.

Now, when it comes to actually seeing the car in person, I encourage you to bring someone along with you who has knowledge of cars or maybe even a mechanic.

Here is a checklist to help you:

2   **Meet The Seller**
- Look at the car in a well-lit area.
- Bring a Diagnostic Scanner to check for engine issues. Diagnostic Scanner tools are $20 on Amazon, but if you don't want to purchase your own, then you can drive the car you're looking at to any Auto Zone nearby. They can scan the car for you for free.
- Look at the body of the car. Are there any dents, dings, scratches? How does the car compare to what it looked like in the photos?
- How are the tires? Are they cracked? How is the tread?
- Open the hood. Does the engine make any loud noises that sound out of place? Do you notice knocking, excessive shaking, or squeaking?

Inspect It First!

2   Meet The Seller

- Is there any oil residue in the engine bay? This could be a major red flag.
- Open the oil cap and check the dipstick. You want your oil to have a syrup-like consistency, not a muddy consistency.
- When on your test drive, how does the car drive? Does it drive straight? Does it accelerate okay?
- When driving, does the car accelerate rapidly (I am talking pedal to the floor). Does the car accelerate as expected?
- Lastly, try sudden braking – brake hard and fast – how does the car stop?

If you don't feel comfortable doing a pre-purchase inspection, take the car to a trusted mechanic and pay to have the car inspected. A pre-purchase inspection could potentially save you thousands later on down the road.

Cash V. Finance

One of the most heated debates within the Turo Host community is whether you should purchase the vehicle in cash or use financing. This really depends on what type of business you'd like to run and what type of cars you're looking to purchase.

Using other people's money (financing) can be the best route for someone who'd like to rent out fairly new cars or maybe luxury cars. Renting newer cars and luxury cars means higher daily rates. Essentially, more profit is being made. Of course, this would require good to excellent credit. You don't want to go this route with poor credit as you'll more than likely pay the highest interest rates, resulting in paying up to double what you bought the car for.

Another thing you'll worry about is the monthly expense of having the car. The cost of renting the car can become quite expensive as now you're not just covering maintenance and insurance, now you need to cover the monthly loan payment. What if the car doesn't rent for a month, maybe 2? You'll still be responsible for the monthly payments due.

If you have great credit and want to get in the business quickly all while using relatively no out-of-pocket, financing is probably the best option for you.

Cash V. Finance

Here are some things to consider when financing:

- Lower repair risk
- Monthly loan payment with possible interest
- Payment is due regardless if the car is rented
- Needs full coverage car insurance
- Lenders have been tracking down cars being used on Turo with personal loans. I have seen host have their cars repossessed because they violated the loan agreements when renting their vehicle, specifically, ALLY Financial.
- More difficult to track profit and losses
- You do not own the title of the car
- Slightly more difficult to sell, especially if your loan is upside down
- More difficult to transfer to the business name
- Maintenance may be less expensive

Cash V. Finance

Here are some things you should know when financing:

- You may pay close to $0 to start the business and make 100% profit if the car rents well
- You'll be able to add a maintenance plan or warranty to your loan
- Financing may result in lenders denying your application if you have too many open loans

If you decide to finance and purchase from a dealership, add the maintenance package. This will save you time and money on maintenance and repairs since repairs are going to be a huge part of running your business.

Cash V. Finance

Here are some things you should know about buying a car in cash:

- Higher repair risk
- No monthly loan payment
- Car insurance is lower because you don't need full coverage
- Once the car has made the money to cover the vehicle purchase cost, it is virtually profit after the maintenance
- No Repossessions. Lenders have been tracking down cars being used on Turo with personal loans. I have seen host have their cars repossessed because they violated the loan agreements when renting their vehicle.
- Easier to track profit and losses
- You own the title of the car
- Easy to sell once the car has reached its max mileage
- Easier to transfer or to purchase with a business name
- Maintenance may be more expensive

Cash V. Finance

Here are some things you should know about buying car cash:

- May take more time to see profit. For example, if you paid $5,000 for the car, you won't really see a profit until the car has made $5,000 in revenue.
- It may take more time to start the business because you'll need to save money
- You can not finance a warranty plan or maintenance plan on the car
- No limit on the cars you can rent. Financing may result in lenders denying your application because you have too many open loans

Cash V. Finance

As I mentioned, this topic is normally a very big debate. Only you know what's the best option for you. Whether you decide to go with cash, financing or maybe both, make sure you look at your long term goal. Will this choice be sustainable? Is this simply a side hustle? Am I going to do this full time? What's my exit strategy? These are all things to consider when deciding finance or cash.

LIST YOUR
Vehicle On Turo

CHAPTER 4

Requirements Before Getting Started:

1. Title

The vehicles you choose must have a clean title. No rebuilt or salvage titles. Turo will deny your car.

2. Age

The vehicle must be 12 years old or newer upon listing.

3. Mileage

Mileage must be under 130,000.

4. Load

The vehicle can not carry more than 8 people (no buses, cargo vans, etc.)

5. Value

An actual cash value of less than $125,000

Listing Your Car On Turo

1. Take Professional Photos

Your vehicle images are the things that will initially grab a potential renter's attention.You'll want a scenic background like a city view, beach view or sometimes even a sun-rise or sun-set view can work to emphasize the car.

Make sure you take at least ten photos. You will need photos of the exterior, interior, front seats, dashboard from the mid-backseat, driver's side, rear and passenger's side and trunk.

Listing Your Car On Turo

2. Information You Need Before The Listing

- Drivers License
- Insurance
- Year
- Make
- Model
- License Plate number
- VIN number

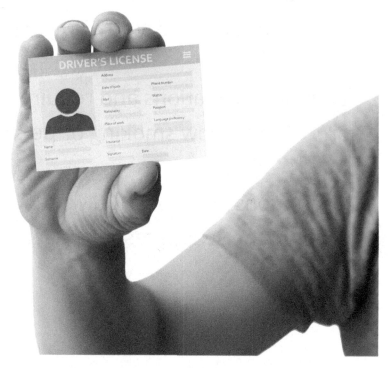

Listing Your Car On Turo

3. Profile Description of The Vehicle

Here is where you'll want to go into details about your car or expectations.

Talk about the unique features your car offers, or options you may offer that other's don't

Discuss what makes your car great. Is your car electric? Does it offer remote start? Do you have no fob entry?

Set your expectations and requirements for handling your car. Will you allow smoking or pets?

Descriptions with over 100 words or 625 characters rank higher in the search results page.

"This lovely 2021 Ford Fusion is a perfect car to take you where you need to go. This car gets great gas mileage and offers features including Bluetooth, cruise control, automatic locks and windows, and USB charging. This car does have some wear and tear on the exterior of the car, but it is an incredible value for the renter on a budget."

Listing Your Car On Turo

4. Introduce Yourself

Fill out your host profile, be sure to introduce yourself by sharing details like why you got into the car sharing business.

People will be more willing to book with someone with great customer service, personality and 5 stars.

Send a pre-written text to your renters. To be welcoming and straight forward with details of delivery etc.

Listing Your Car On Turo

5. Pricing

Pricing is adjustable, and can be automized by Turo. If you decide to automize your pricing, Turo allows you to choose an allowable minimum and maximum price. According to the market Turo will fluctuate the price.

You may also want to see what other cars in your area cost and then rent your car for something similar (or even $1-$2 lower to attract more renters at the beginning).

TURO HOST
Protection Plan
Options

CHAPTER 5

Protection Plans Available

The last step of the process of renting your car on Turo is choosing your insurance coverage. This is important because it will dictate how much you will earn each trip and how much coverage you will have in case of an accident or total loss of your vehicle. Accidents do happen, so it is important to be covered.

Turo offers five different host protection plans. Following is a brief rundown of Turo insurance coverage directly from Turo's website:

60 Plan	70 Plan	75 Plan
Earn 60% of the trip price	Earn 70% of the trip price	Earn 75% of the trip price
Up to $750,000 in third-party liability insurance	Up to $750,000 in third-party liability insurance	Up to $750,000 in third-party liability insurance
Turo pays 100% of eligible damage costs	Turo pays 100% of eligible damage costs above the deductible	Turo pays 100% of eligible damage costs above the deductible
No deductible	$250 deductible	$750 deductible
Includes exterior wear and tear reimbursement	$30/day replacement vehicle reimbursement during repair (10 day max)	No replacement vehicle reimbursement during repair
Includes loss of hosting income during repair OR $50/day replacement vehicle reimbursement (10 day max)	Doesn't include exterior wear and tear reimbursement or hosting income during repair	Doesn't include exterior wear and tear reimbursement or hosting income during repair

80 Plan	85 Plan
Earn 80% of the trip price	Earn 85% of the trip price
Up to $750,000 in third-party liability insurance	Up to $750,000 in third-party liability insurance
Turo pays 100% of eligible damage costs above the deductible	Turo pays 100% of eligible damage costs above the deductible
$1,625 deductible	$2,500 deductible
No replacement vehicle reimbursement during repair	No replacement vehicle reimbursement during repair
Doesn't include exterior wear and tear reimbursement or hosting income during repair	Doesn't include exterior wear and tear reimbursement or hosting income during repair

GETTING YOUR
Car On The Road

CHAPTER 6

GETTING YOUR CAR ON THE ROAD

Clean Car

The first step in prepping your car for a rental is to make sure the car is clean and running smoothly. Make sure there are no mechanical issues with the car prior to the rental.

This can be as simple as vacuuming the car and wiping it down with disinfectant or it can be as detailed as taking it to a car wash.

GETTING YOUR CAR ON THE ROAD

Take Photos

Per the Turo Terms of Service (HIGHLY recommend you read), you need to take photos of the car before and after the rental for you to be covered under insurance. 24 hours or less before the rental, make sure to take photos of the car. Take pictures of EVERYTHING! Tires, trunk, dashboard, seats, roof, everything!

Once you have taken these photos you will upload them to the app. You will also want to note the gas level of the car as well as the odometer reading on the car.

GETTING YOUR CAR ON THE ROAD

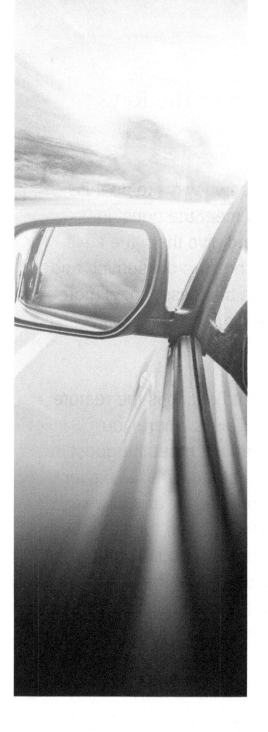

Confirm Guest Identity

You could ask the guest to send you photos of their ID along with a selfie photo of them holding their ID next to their face. You could also meet the guest in person before the rental and confirm their ID in person.

Whichever route you choose, it is crucial to confirm the identity and eligibility of the person who is renting your car. Basically, you'll want to make sure the person who is renting your car is the same person who owns the Turo account that rented your car. This needs to be done no more than 24 hours before the rental.

GETTING YOUR CAR ON THE ROAD

Hand Over the Keys

There are two ways to do this. One is to meet the guest in person and give them the keys. This can be time-consuming and make this business model more of a job and less of a passive revenue stream.

The second option is the remote method. This is where you actually do not meet the guest in person. Instead, you have a lockbox system set up at your car, and when it is time for the guest to get the keys, you give them the lockbox code, the guest grabs the keys, and they are all set.

WINNING TIPS FOR YOUR TURO BUSINESS

RESPONSE

Be responsive, respond to trip requests and changes as soon as you can.

DELIVERY FEE

Always charge a delivery fee (Airport, Transit station etc.

DO YOUR HOMEWORK!

You don't want to under sell your vehicle. I highly recommend researching how the same vehicle your renting is doing in your market and rent your's out for slightly lower in order to get started and get some ratings.

WINNING TIPS FOR YOUR TURO BUSINESS

CANCELLATIONS

No cancellations for the first month of being a turo host
is cruical. Turo charges a $100 cancellation fee.
If the car is in maintenance or unavailable please take
the days off the calendar. As a Turo host your
performance is being monitored and you will be
reviewed to achieve All star host status. Cancellations
can lower your vehicle search ranking and removal from
Turo platform.

OFFERING DISCOUNTS

Turo opts all vehicle listings into offering discounts. I
would carefully consider the monthly/weekly discounts
and only pick one discount for a more safe profit
margin.

WINNING TIPS FOR YOUR TURO BUSINESS

EXTRAS

Extras are relatively new features that Turo has introduced to the platform. Take a look at the list of features and see which ones are applicable for your area. Beach chairs, beach towels, and coolers are going to be in high demand in Miami/ Ft. Lauderdale. A child car seat may be popular for large SUVs. Find out which extras you can offer at a profitable price.

WINNING TIPS FOR YOUR TURO BUSINESS

CONTACTLESS DELIVERY

If you're like me, or don't have much time to deliver the vehicle to the guest, you can offer contactless delivery. This means you'll be parking the car in a safe area and the guest will retrieve the car without your presence.

There are a couple things you'll may want to purchase prior to offering this:

- A window lockbox to place the keys (amazon)
- A faraday bag for the FOB (amazon)

You'll want to place the FOB in the faraday bag and then place the bag inside of the lockbox. The faraday bag will prevent any signals coming from the key to the car. If you have a car with keyless entry, you'll definitely be needing this.

WINNING TIPS FOR YOUR TURO BUSINESS

PRECAUTIONS

Lastly, you want to make sure you take every precaution possible to protect your asset, the vehicle. You may want to consider placing a GPS into the car. I use GoldStar on my own vehicle as the GPS is hardwired into the car, out of plain sight, and it offers a kill switch. You want to make sure that if a thief is trying to steal your car, they will not have the ability to pull the GPS out of the car in plain sight. Another thing you want to consider is the kill switch. A kill switch simply means that you'll be able to shut off the engine from a click of a button. If a thief has not returned your car, you'll be able to turn the kill switch on and repossess the car. Gold Star offers both.

RETURNING THE
Vehicle

CHAPTER 7

Returning The Vehicle

Step 1:
The Guest Returns The Car

Once the rental is over, the guest will return the car, typically to the same location they picked it up at. This is the end of the rental.

Step 2:
Take Photos of the Car and Log Gas/Mileage

Within 24 hours (no later!), you will need to go to the car, take photos of the car, and inspect it for any damage. The app will prompt you to do this once the guest checks out. If there are any damages, this will need to be reported and documented to Turo within 24 Hours.

You will then log mileage and gas to ensure that the gas levels were returned to where they were pre-rental (the guest is responsible for gas), and you will need to ensure the guest did not go over the mileage limit. The app will prompt you to enter this information.

If the car is returned without the proper amount of gas, over allowed mileage or tolls/parking tickets, you could be eligible for reimbursement.

Make sure to keep all proof and keep an eye for any notices in the mail for tolls or parking tickets. You can file for reimbursement on the Turo App by filing an invoice.

CAR SHARING
Business Expenses

CHAPTER 8

Car Sharing Business Expenses

Like any business, a peer-to-peer car sharing business model has costs. Here are some typical expenses of a Turo fleet:

1 Insurance

Whether you are running a side hustle with your personal car or a business under an LLC your vehicle(s) will need insurance that follow your state guidelines. The cost of this will be dictated by the car and your own driving record.

2 Maintenance

Maintenance will be due on any vehicle, new or old. Oil changes, and tire changes will be the most common, but for older vehicles, you may need to give the car more attention.

3 Repairs

Accidents may happen, and if they do, you want to be prepared. Make sure to have a saving for each rental car encase they need to be repaired.

4 Parking

Depending on where you store your vehicles for your guest, you may need to rent commercial parking, especially at the airport. If you have multiple cars you may want to consider renting a commercial lot to store them when they're not being rented.

Car Sharing Business Expenses

For the most part, the cost of doing business will mostly come down to storage (if applicable), insurance, maintenance, and repairs. The cost of these items will be dictated by what car you have and who rents your vehicles.

For example, a Honda is going to have significantly less maintenance cost than a BMW.

If you have purchased your vehicle from a dealership with a loan, I would highly recommend adding a maintenance package to the vehicle, as this will keep maintenance cost low.

The last hidden expense you should keep in mind is depreciation. If you buy cars at the depreciation bottom (as mentioned earlier), depreciation is not much of an issue. But if you buy cars brand new, depreciation will be a massive cost that will eat into your bottom line.

Car Sharing Business Expenses

Further discussing maintenance, it isn't uncommon to have to do maintenance more often than you would normally because your cars are being driven much more frequently, and it isn't entirely uncommon for cars to be abused on rentals.... sorry but it's the truth.

Below are the most common maintenance issues that will come up with your cars:

- Oil & Filter Changes

- Alignment. Tires will become unaligned as guests may hit curbs and potholes in your cars, especially if you're in the city. This isn't something you will need to do all the time, but expect to do it multiple times a year.

- Tires. Tires get worn more quickly when they are being used more often.

- Suspension Components

These are just a few examples of the maintenance issues that could come up with your Turo vehicles. All the costs associated with these maintenance issues will be dictated by the type of the vehicle.

Car Sharing Business Expenses

As for repairs, well it's bond to happen at some point. Guests will damage your cars. It isn't a matter of if, it's mostly a matter of when.

When it comes to damage to your vehicle, as long as you have done your part in protecting yourself with Turo rentals (i.e., following the terms of service), then you will be covered, and you should be reimbursed when it comes to any Turo damage.

Depending on the type of damage you have to your car, you may need to take the car to a shop, or you could try to repair the car yourself. You should be reimbursed for any damage that does occur (but cases do vary, so read the terms of service!).

TURO
Must Haves

CHAPTER 9

1. Battery charger, jump start kit for emergency use.
2. Start a car wash kit (portable vacuum, tire cleaner, interior spray, etc.)
3. GPS tracker with kill switch
4. Ozone Odor Eliminator (you'll need this if a guest smokes in the car. Turo has a strict policy on smoking and allows you to collect a smoking fee if you have proof that the guest has smoked in the car.)
5. Have more than one set of keys
6. Find a mobile mechanic and glass repair specialist.

PROMOTING YOUR
Business Off
The Turo App

CHAPTER 10

Turo is not the only place you can promote your car rental business. Here are some other ways you can market your business:

Promoting Your Business Off The Turo App

Promotional Items

Social Media

Create A Website

Photographers

Promoting Your Business Off The Turo App

Video Directors

Customer Contact

Referrals

Car Magnets

CONCLUSION

This process I have discussed is easier said than done. There will be challenges in car sharing with Turo but this applies to any business.

There are always issues that come up with any side hustle and car sharing with Turo is no different. The best thing any car sharing host can do for themselves and their business is to know the terms of service.

Always know what you are getting into when it comes to Turo, know and understand the rules, know what you need to do to be protected — this is so incredibly important.

Turo is a wonderful side hustle, and car-sharing is a great and lucrative business model. I truly believe that anyone can succeed at it. It really comes down to just a few steps:

- Know the terms of service.
- Buy cars at the right price.
- Follow the process.

If you do this, you can truly start a side hustle that can convert to a 6 figure business.

Made in the USA
Las Vegas, NV
24 November 2024

12579553R00044